Intro

Fascinating. In fact, hysterically entertaining at times…
Humans in the workplace!

I infiltrated this harried, frenzied
environment over 26 years ago
because there was such a buzz
about it in the world where I come from.
That would be Jurdy World. Nice to meet you, I'm Jurdy.

Believing I exist might be a stretch for you since you're pretty
wrapped up in your own world much less thinking about another
world. But where I come from, we think big. There is no gender,
age, class, culture or race defining traits that inhibit our ability to be
successful at work. We all support each other, work in unison, and
most of all we work smart – really smart. That's why we were so
surprised when we started hearing noise about how you did things.
There were rumors flying around about your 24 hour work days, 15
minute lunch breaks, back stabbing, mistakes, mental ruts, failure
to prepare, complaining all the time, blaming others, and just running
in circles.

And so the assignment came to me one day from "Jurdy Resources"
(our equivalent of a "human resources" department, go figure) to
go and observe humans in the workplace to see if there were any
best practices worth looking at which we just hadn't considered. It
seemed hard to believe there would be based on all we had heard,
but in Jurdy World, we never take things for granted and we always
see what we can learn from others.

So I began my observations of humans in the workplace in 1980
and through the years you were oblivious to being watched. Oblivion
oft-times seems to be a common trait at your work. Since then, this
Jurdy journey has spanned companies from small local businesses
to an international Fortune 500 corporation, from clerical jobs to
management positions, from grass roots philosophies to corporate-
wide brain washing.

Yes, I discovered that many of these rumors were true, but there was something I hadn't expected. I was amazed at how incredibly talented and creative you really are! The workplace pitfalls aren't indicative of humans themselves, but rather their approach to work. Humans are smart, but the way they oft-times work isn't. You have so much ingenuity but you're so far from geniuses when it comes to collaborating and applying all the tools you have available to you in other humans and technology. But in the end, I do conclude: You are advanced beings.

Upon submitting my findings at the end of my 26 year assignment, the Jurdy Lama, our wisest Jurdy, suggested I share this feedback in the hopes of showing you how much you have going for you– that with some tweaking and strong forethought, you could thrive at work as individuals and as teams. So here is my book, albeit a short book because of your famous short attention spans. Since humans typically thrive on immediate gratification, I wrote fast and efficient tips (ones that we use) to improve your career, work environment and those impossible work relationships! You know the ones I mean – it gets ugly, doesn't it?

Throughout this book I point out my observations of your **Current World**… and then I offer you tips and advice on the Jurdy World way, **Jurdy's Target World**. If this Target World were studied and adopted by humans, your achievements, personal happiness and morale would increase beyond your wildest human dreams. You would be excited, motivated and empowered. In fact, let's just say work would …"rock"!

What else should you know before reading this book?

In Jurdy World, we take the health of our environment very seriously. Ironically enough, I'm green on the outside and I'm also green on the inside. And yes, I will help you get green for your earth environment so you can go from global warming to global greening… but first things first. We need to focus on the task at hand of getting employees and companies to focus on a better, stronger more efficient workplace. Once you nail this, you will be ready to GET GREENING!

(intro continues one more page – keep going!)

Keep this in mind also: The core value in Jurdy World is laughter. We laugh at ourselves and at life because the ability to do so keeps you loose, keeps you fresh and gives you perspective, while actually maximizing your performance! Given the importance of laughter, I added in Jurdy cartoons reflecting human situations to show you how pertinent humor can be even when you are talking about serious topics.

After finishing my assignment on earth, The Jurdy Lama asked me if a human would be good in our work force, you know, a valuable team member. My response was, "…but why should I hire a human?". Right now, all I have is that question… but the answer doesn't have to be worlds away.

Jurdy

Caution:
There will be no quiz on the following content. However, if you fail to exercise these tips, you may remain stagnant, depressed and ineffective in the workplace.

Disclaimer:
Residents of Jurdy World and it's subsidiary planets take no responsibility for the human adoption … or denial… of the contents contained herein. We only hope to influence those less brilliant than ourselves.

Jurdy™

www.jurdy.net

Jurdy World Get Smart Sections

Jurdy™

"I tried the human thing of 'keeping my eye out' for something, but when opportunity came along, I couldn't see it."

Jurdy, 2007

(why not be alert to all things all the time?)

Give Yourself a Promotion

You are your only boss.

Your Current World

The Blame Game

Human workers blame other human workers for their lack of success, recognition and promotions. You blame others whenever things don't work out for you as if you are helpless, not responsible and held "workplace hostage" in your stagnant situation.

The Envy Game

You're scared to be happy for other and their success. Somehow you think if you are happy for them, they'll do better than you. You rarely congratulate, recognize or share in another co-worker's accomplishments… you envy them.

The Complain Game

Gripe, whine, complain… this happens a lot and it's a bad non-productive habit. You complain to others to make yourself feel better. Sometimes you even call these complainers "leaders". We would call them "flat tires" because they keep the team from going anywhere.

Jurdy's Target World

Blaming others for your lack of movement, recognition or promotions is only creating more negative energy. I guess you'd say "It's human" to blame everyone or everything else for your troubles at work, but it's really humanly impossible for them to control your success. By blaming other people and other things, you give them all the power that you in fact already have to get your situation turned around.

In Jurdy World, each individual recognizes that *only we* can control our own destiny. We each take full responsibility for our success, failures and all that junk in between. If we aren't happy with someone or something, we *focus only on what we have control over*. We look at our options, weigh things out, explore alternatives, brainstorm and we keep looking for ways to "move the ball." Even by just inching the ball along, eventually an individual can create enough change to … change… their situation. Put your energy into your own success and results will start to happen. Positive energy yields positive results 2:1.

So how can you stop throwing blame and move towards fame? Glad you asked.

Break the habit of blaming others. The less you blame others from this point forward, the more you gain mentally to put towards all that is positive which you can attract.

Sell yourself! If someone is "holding you back" or is "in your way" … just go around them. A human worker gets to where they are because another human knows about them, thinks about them or heard about them. Don't rely on a co-worker – sell yourself to everyone you can, here's how:

Track your accomplishments. Give them to your supervisor, to their supervisor and the next supervisor up. If no one requests your list of accomplishments, all the more reason to track and submit them. If you take your work seriously, so will your management and peers.

Get visibility! Don't let someone else do the talking for your career. Distribute industry related articles and "cc" the world on them! Put "fyi" and your name at the top before making copies. Just seeing your name regularly gets you critical subliminal recognition. Be seen. Hang out where the important people hang out. (I think you refer to them as "management").

Act today what you want to be tomorrow. If you want to be a leader tomorrow, start assuming assignments that require leadership skills *today*. If you want to get a promotion, start doing more than what is expected *today*. Acting today what you want to be tomorrow takes your focus off of blaming others for what you don't have and puts the focus back on you… where it should be. So many times I watched you get upset because you didn't get a promotion for the job you were doing today and you blamed others. In Jurdy World, we get a promotion for what *extra* we are doing that warrants being recognized to that next level. Interesting. Do more, give more, see more, hear more, try more… then watch yourself move more! Don't focus on others getting ahead… just start "getting ahead of yourself" to get ahead.

4

One of the most disappointing things I found in the human workplace was how difficult it is for you to be happy for other co-workers in their accomplishments. Even though the workplace requires team players, you still seem to make it all about *you*.

In Jurdy World, it's not all about *me*, it's not all about *you*, it's about *success*. In your world, it's each man or woman for him- or herself, even when it's at the expense of others. In Jurdy World, we know we can't achieve success without each other. Humans seem to think that the happier you are for a co-worker, the better that co-worker will do and consequently the worse you'll do. In Jurdy World, the better a co-worker does, the stronger the whole team becomes. Humans are most comfortable in an egocentric work environment and yet ironically, if you truly had strong egos you would not operate out of fear like you do. In Jurdy World, we never let ourselves get too comfortable acting without the input of others, recognizing that our team environment keeps us each challenged, alert and informed. Okay, so now what?

In three simple steps you can stop this envy thing.

Turn their success into your success. The better you make others look, the better they will look upon you. Congratulate, celebrate and recognize others. Even if you don't believe in this, start doing it. This is a highly beneficial habit to get into. Trust me. As they move along they will want to bring you along with them… or as you move along, they will want to come with you. Either way, it's success for you both.

Build teams and stop working in a vacuum. Start to build your own teams. Identify those you work with who are the most motivated, positive and energetic. Try to pull them in on tasks you have and ask them for their ideas. Watch how much stronger your end result is and how much more rewarding your work day will become. Teams keep your work exciting, your ideas sharp and your relationships strong.

Get involved and partake. You will be less envious of others if you get involved in projects and special assignments with them. Not only is this motivational, you'll also find you are inherently more supportive of your co-workers because you developed a working relationship with them as you completed the tasks together. Remember, envy makes enemies. So…

See who needs help and volunteer. Get your envy turned around by changing your behavior. Dive in and voluntarily help your co-workers. Involvement = Ingenuity.

Be thankful for what you have. You've heard the phrase "green with envy?" (I'm particularly fond of green.) Well, stop envying others and start being thankful for what *you* have to offer. Better things will come when you can do this.

Encourage, don't envy. Push others to do well and succeed. When the bosses see you doing this, you may jump leaps and bounds into higher positions because you've shown you can corral the troops! Companies need humans that can do that because so few are actually capable of producing that result!

Humans love to complain! Sorry if I sound like I'm complaining. These human bouts of complaining, referred to as "bitch sessions," are usually facilitated by the "bitch master." It doesn't take much to earn this position. You have to find the negative in everything, point it out and recruit others to do the same.

©Jenifer Jurden 2006

This cartoon is particularly large because this problem is so incredibly prevalent throughout the human workplace. Negative people don't like to lead, they just love followers. You have a saying "misery loves company" but in Jurdy World, companies don't tolerate misery.

A company complainer is a company drainer. Complainers are leaks of profitability because they are counter-productive. If someone needs confirmation as to what *can't* be done, these are their "go to" people. Common words out of their mouths are: "I can't." "How can they ask us to do this." "We'll never get this done." "No way." and "If they think I'm doing this, they're crazy." In the Target World, the only complaining should be about the workers who engage in this behavior.

Okay, enough complaining. Let's talk about gaining.

Be positive or be quiet. If things are really bad at work, your co-workers already know it and don't need it pointed out again. Start being positive NOW!! Try to refrain from partaking in any negative talk and see how fast the complainers abandon you. This is the most critical step to getting yourself to a more positive and visible place. If you can't be positive, just be quiet. Start a list of all the positive things you have going for you at work. Go ahead, you can do it!

Re-align yourself with optimists. You know the expression "you are what you eat." Well, in Jurdy World, ours is "you are whom you hang out with." If you hang with negative people, you'll become more negative. If you hang with the positive ones, the movers and shakers, you'll go places. Ask them to lunch, go for drinks. Start getting to know them. Positive thinkers brainstorm. Complainers brainwash. Anyone can be positive when things are going well - it's these optimists who know how to be positive even when things get rough.

Model yourself after the ones who get it right. You are usually so busy worrying about what others think of you that you don't take the time to notice others. In the Target World, you learn from the best role models you have exposure to. Pay attention. Not unlike school, the workplace can teach you invaluable lessons if you have an open mind. Observe, learn and put it all into motion.

Identify the top 5 positive leaders you know in your company and start to study their behavior. What makes them positive? How do they show others they are optimistic? What motivates them? How do they interact with the complainers? Take notes, take action, make changes. Your results will be … positive!

Hit the Human Lotto!

Get along with others and get going.

Your Current World

Little respect for respect.

From what I can see, human workers show little respect for each other, particularly their management. Not a smart move. By failing to show respect, you are telling others that they have nothing to offer you. All they'll see are your poor listening skills, inappropriate behavior and a belief that you have nothing to learn. That would mean you have things to learn!

Relationships are discarded not developed.

Often, you don't develop relationships with others, you discard them. There is little effort to help others develop and form strong foundations on which to build a winning team. Learn to create and support leadership in one another and start getting the most out of each person.

Motivation is missing.

Human workers are severely lacking motivation. Does robotic mean anything to you? You go to work each day and "go through the motions" but those motions don't really take you very far, since there is little spark, enthusiasm or excitement. If you get into gear you'll turn those motions into magic.

Jurdy's Target World

Pay respect to respect

Underestimating respect is a huge career limiting move. If you don't respect others, they won't respect you. This is definitely where *you get what you give* applies. Your co-workers, particularly your management (you know, the hand that feeds you), need to feel that they matter and that you acknowledge all they have to offer. Take note, the people you don't respect will know it, and even more importantly, they'll remember it. This could bite you in the …. well, you know. If you want others to take you seriously, you have to take them more seriously.

In Jurdy World, we recognize the power of respect and use it to our advantage. BIG advantage. We respect our management as much as we can because they are ultimately responsible for our career. This works for us because then we get all that respect back. At the end of the day, that means money in our pockets and smiles on our faces. We listen to what others have to say, another strong sign of respect. We convey the fact that we all have something to learn from each other. By sharing information we are smarter as individuals, sharper as teams. To be respected feels good… but to pay respect is just *smart*.

Yeah, yeah… but what does this all mean for you?

Listen and acknowledge others. When others offer up ideas or opinions, make good eye contact and refrain from offering input until you have heard what *they* have to say. Don't cut them off, don't speak your mind until you pay mind to what they have said. They will return the favor, trust me. When others speak up, listen up!

Be appropriate and mind your manners. You may not believe this, but manners matter. How you conduct yourself does not go unnoticed. Your actions, your manner of speaking, your body language, your behavior... it all matters A LOT. Every move you make and word you speak is what you are measured by… So never say or do something you'll regret later.

Learn you've got something to learn from others. One of the biggest lessons you can learn is that there's always something you can learn. And that's probably one of the most important things your co-workers and management have to offer you. To think you can't learn anything from them is short-sighted, egocentric and career-limiting. Instead, try the Jurdy Way by soaking up as much knowledge as you can even from the ones you don't like. Let your co-workers know you are ready to learn whatever they have to offer. This will open doors with others, and the more doors you open with others, the more places you can go. If you shut others out, you shut yourself out of advancement.

Develop relationships and reap.

Relationships are the foundation of any success you hope to achieve. Human interaction is the fuel for business and personal survival. Humans may think they don't need each other to succeed, when in fact, how well you get along with others influences how well you'll do in your job. It's all about getting outside of your own skin and making connections with other co-workers. *Each and every one.* Humans are big on analogies, so try this one out: Imagine that each person is a rung on your career ladder. Step too hard and you break a rung. This slows or stops your climb. Take care in climbing and you'll make it to the top. Each and every co-worker has the ability to influence your job, be it today or down the road. Don't underestimate the power of relationships. Also, don't be afraid to connect with those you're not sure about – each connection is an opportunity, even if you can't see it at first.

In Jurdy World we don't hire anyone who doesn't value other workers and acknowledge how critical relationships are. In fact, we have a saying, "We hire Jurdys who like other Jurdys." During the interview process, we ask the tough question: "What would you do if you were forced to work with someone you thought to be impossible?" The answer we look for is "I'd work hard to find ways to work with them." Keeping your friends close and your enemies even closer applies to the workplace big time! I made this section longer because it's an area which needs a lot of work.

Avoid the Gossip Gala. Assume what you say about co-workers can and will get back to them. Gossip is a workplace cancer and will eat away at your reputation, your work and your team. Getting along with others means getting beyond the pettiness that humans so often succumb to. In Jurdy World, the only time we are allowed to talk about another is when we recognize them for a job well done. Focus on the activities about the work, not the chit-chat about the workers. Mind your own business and don't be bullied into talking about others.

Treat each individual individually. Simply put, no two people are the same. Just like you don't wear the same clothes in hot weather as you do in cold, your approach to co-workers should be equally versatile. Adopt and utilize different styles for different personalities. Whatever makes each one tick… tick that way. Here's how: Don't just look at *what* they do, look at *why* they do what they do. Identifying why they work the way they do will provide you with answers on how to best work with them. Adapt to the way others work and look at what motivates them, down to the individual level. You'll be amazed at what a difference this makes in your effectiveness.

Okay, so how do you build relationships with co-workers, even the ones you can't stand?

Pinpoint the Personalities. Understanding who your co-workers are and what makes them tick is first and foremost. I know many of you have read complicated text-book definitions of various personality types. But in Jurdy World, we label ours in a user friendly fashion so we can actually remember them and use them to our advantage. Here goes:

The *"We We We's"* These are the healthiest work specimens. They are all about teamwork, they motivate and they realize that everyone has a part in the end result. They strive for team and company success. They win big time.

The *"Me Me Me's"* These are the egocentric specimens. Not as likely to be leaders, although some do make it through, they only care about themselves and have difficulty working in a team environment. They seek solo success and can get it.

The *"See See See's"* This is the most complacent species but they oft-times can be the work horses of the organization. They are not aggressive and don't care about advancement, rather they watch as others pass them by. These specimens are critical because you need to have good workers who are happy just getting the work out – that's their success.

The **"Hee Hee Hee's"** These are the sliest specimens around. You can hear them cackling as they attempt to undermine everything you do so they'll get all the glory. They are commonly known as "backstabbers." You need to pay the closest attention to and work the hardest with this personality type. Destroying other's successes is what they base their success on… and they'll stop at nothing. They can't be trusted because they don't trust others. They twist the facts, love playing the victim and will eventually turn on others who had previously helped them out. They are loyal only to themselves. They are most comfortable when they can pull you into their frenzied world. It makes them feel like they are in control of you and your success. Prove them wrong.

Here are bonus Jurdy World tips for dealing with the four types of personalities. Pay attention… it's good stuff.

"We We We's"

Work as closely as you can with this type of personality. Support them, get on their team and adopt the best of their traits. They get things done, they get strong results and that's exactly who you want to be like and be aligned with. Learn what you can from them and give them all you've got. They'll remember you on their way up. Trust the hell out of them.

"Me Me Me's"

Like it or not, like *them* or not, you need to learn to work well with them. The secret: *Initially make it all about them.* They won't care about you until you show you care about them. Feed their egos, listen to them and show them respect. Once they feel less threatened, feel that you understand them, their guard will come down and they'll start letting you in. This is what you want because they're often the ones who know how to get visibility for themselves and advance. If you go to bat for them, they'll eventually go to bat for you. If you don't go to bat for them…. watch out.

"See See See's"

This is the forgotten group, often overlooked or taken for granted. "Loyal" is their name and production is their game. Focus on rewarding this group as much as possible to keep them motivated and productive. They are essentially harmless; they just want to do their job. They don't care about promotions, advancement or management positions. They're just happy to sit and watch as others move up the ladder. Recognize their contributions and be thankful they show up every day. They like taking direction and getting the job done. But caution – they rarely feel comfortable making decisions on their own.

"Hee Hee Hee's"

This is the most dangerous group. Read carefully. These people are not what they seem, and are what they don't seem. That makes it all the more difficult to create a good working relationship with them. They could care less about relationships... *except when one will benefit them directly*. They'll lie, deceive and do whatever it takes to win. They believe their distortions but will deny them just as easily.

Here are some things you can do to help you succeed with them. The relationship may never be great, but it will certainly be better than the relationships others have with them:

- *Keep them at arm's length.* Deal with them only when you have to.
- *Don't try to be friends.* They may try to be friends with you when they need something. Don't fall for it. Keep your interactions professional and "work only" focused.
- *Don't gossip about them or with them.* You'll hang yourself. Keep a clean record with them. Don't give them anything they can use against you.
- *Behave as professionally and consistently as you can.* They love to intimidate. Never let on! No matter how hard it is, never give up your emotions to them. Be a rock. **Good luck!**

Motivating others is the secret to being a true leader. It's a sure-fire way to get noticed! Motivated workers are totally unstoppable. They go above and beyond and do whatever it takes to win. If the workers are the cars in the race, motivation is the gasoline. One needs the other to win. One of the biggest pitfalls I see in your companies is that you put people in leadership positions who are not motivators. This is a major oversight and one you will pay for dearly. One thing you can count on: if the team isn't motivated, the team will let you know one way or the other, and innovation and productivity will suffer.

In Jurdy World, there are three steps to motivation: One, motivate *yourself*. Two, motivate *co-workers*. Three, motivate your *management*. All managers must be motivators, no exceptions. Everyone we interview is evaluated for their ability to motivate. (We even look to see how well they motivate the interviewer.) Motivation is not a science, it's an art. Be creative, be original and be consistent. Here we go…

Motivate yourself. Others can help motivate you, but only you are responsible for your own motivation. Knowing what motivates you is the first step to being happy and productive. Be it the money, the people, the company, the benefits. Identify what motivates you and keep your eye on it during those challenging times. The more motivated you are, the more successful you'll be. At the end of the day, it is your motivation that will help you stand out from others. So get motivated, not upset with others when *you* can't get into motion.

Motivate co-workers. While you are not responsible for another's motivation, you can most definitely influence them. The better you are at motivating others the better your career will be. Motivating others means getting the most out of them. This leads to high creativity, productivity and job satisfaction. Everyone's happy under your clock! Speak their language. If someone is aggressive, be assertive. If someone is shy, approach them carefully. If someone has difficulty communicating, try reaching them creatively through emails, memos or a voicemail before you do a face to face. Also remember: reward, reward, reward. From a thank you to a bonus, from a card to a free lunch, from an equipment upgrade to a "great job at that meeting!" Oh, and don't forget to celebrate work anniversaries and birthdays. Rewarding others will be more than rewarding for you. Trust me on this one.

Motivate your management. This is one major use of motivational skills that most humans don't recognize. Motivating those around you and under you is customary, but motivating your *management* could be the secret to your success. Most do not see this treasure-trove of opportunity. Just like managers are expected to be motivators, they too are only human (no pun intended) and need others to fuel their motivation. That includes those whose efforts they manage. Show excitement about their work, give them kudos when they do a good job, give them a card on boss's day. When you see they are having a bad day, ask what you can do to help. Help them look good and feel good about the work coming out of you and your team. Keep your eye on the boss and they in turn will keep their eye on you.

Human 911

Human health and attitude... live, laugh and lunge!

Your Current World

You have no life.

Many human workers are alive but have no life. Not only do you work more than you live, you live to work. With little to no balance in your lives, you can become counter-productive and stale. You see co-workers more than you do friends and family. So, where's the fun? Somewhere, sometime someone told you *life must be intense and serious*. Not funny.

Your bodies take a beating.

Your bodies go through more in a year than ours do in a lifetime. You deprive them of sleep, exercise and nutrition. You miss a doctor's appointment for a meeting and lose a night's sleep for a presentation. The problem isn't that this is the exception, the problem is that it's the norm.

Your minds are on cruise control.

You pay no mind to your minds. You operate on cruise control and ignore the very things your mind requires to stay sharp. If your mind is a terrible thing to waste, why waste your mind on terrible things? You feed your bodies, but you don't feed your minds. Humans bypass the time needed for spirituality, education and peace ... of mind.

 25

Jurdy's Target World

Get a life!

Having a life brings "life" to everything you do. By life, I mean awareness of your existence, enjoying the journey along the way. This means taking time, having time and enjoying time. Having fun is the door to happiness and perspective to manage all other facets of your human existence. A knee-slapping, hysterical laugh can cure just about anything you have going on. That saying "laugh to keep from crying" is lost on 90% of the work force when it should be mandatory. Fun is fun … absolutely go ahead and have a "wild hair".

In Jurdy World, we need to have a life to live. We pay attention to balance and make sure the scales don't tip too far in one direction. Our families see us more than our co-workers, we make time to do nothing (you call it "down-time") and we laugh our - - -s off. A practical joke is worth its weight in gold in Jurdy World. Some of our best ideas and efforts have come from joking around. When we can be happy at work, we are… happy working. In Jurdy World, our life is our life. We call that living!

Laugh your buns off. For whatever reason, laughter is oft-times frowned upon in your companies, when in reality humor is a stress-reliever and perspective-giver. Fun keeps workers loyal and builds relationships necessary to carry you through trying times. Fun is the top core value in Jurdy World because it promotes creativity, longevity and excitement. A burst of laughter can yield an outbreak of great ideas. And practical jokes and laughter can increase productivity so long as you don't take the pranks too far.

Get your down time up. Making time to do nothing is a huge something! Humans completely miss the benefit of "downtime". It's rejuvenating and inspiring. Doing nothing can help you catch your breath from the mayhem, while preparing you for the frenzy to come. It allows you to live, not just exist. With down time you are able to notice the small details of your surroundings and relationships. You find joy in the smaller things and that joy re-fuels you for the rest.

Get to know your family and friends again. You may not acknowledge this, but if there's one thing you need, it's strong relationships with friends and family. Not only do they offer support and guidance, but they are also the fabric of who you are, and who you can become. Bonding with others outside of the work place is critical to the balance you need. Treat your friends like family and your family like friends. Enjoy them, appreciate them and let them love you as we do each other in Jurdy World. We know the importance of feeding these relationships because they are with us for the long haul. It's these very connections that give us the foundation and strength to endure the unpredictable and the unreliable. They ground us, feed us and sustain us. It's comforting to know that even when they can't be with us, they are.

P.S. Don't think that making work a priority at the expense of your relationships is worth it. I know this sounds harsh but with or without you, work will go on. Enjoying your life outside of work is essential to a healthy existence.

Beef up your bodies!

Your bodies are your vehicle in this life. Just as your car needs tune-ups, so does your body. As far as I know, human bodies don't come with a lifetime guarantee. And not unlike cars, your body can only run on empty for so long. It needs fluids, maintenance, occasional repairs. Pay attention to your body's signals and give it what it needs before it falls apart.

In Jurdy World we recognize that it's much easier to stay in shape than to play "catch-up" when it's all gone awry. The better shape you're in, the better shape you're in to manage the daily stresses at work. Humans don't realize the toll stress takes on their physical and mental well-being. We have three absolute requirements: Sleep enough, exercise enough and eat healthy enough. Just like everything else, you get what you give. Okay, blah, blah, blah. So what should you do?

Get smart, get sleep. Sleep is nature's energy pill. It fills the tank, lights the fire and gets us moving. Often, humans don't see the importance of getting the rest required to fully function and many of you have trouble sleeping because you can't shut off your brain. While you think you may get more done by losing sleep, eventually you'll get nothing done when you crash and burn.

© Jenifer Jurden 2006   www.jurdy.net

Exercise for energy. Exercise and energy reign in Jurdy World: Activity = Acuity = Longevity. Exercise is just as important to schedule as any meeting or appointment. No matter how unmotivated you may be to exercise, do it anyway. While getting started may be hard, you will feel and reap the benefits. Keep your bodies moving to keep your ideas sharp. In Jurdy World a lot of our ideas and perspective come to us while we work out. Exercise your body to wake up your ideas!

Be mindful of your mind. The human mind is underrated and underused. And yet, it's also in overdrive just trying to keep up with the stress and drama you regularly put it through. Just like your body, you need to feed your mind. In Jurdy World, we have three ways to keep our minds well nourished.

One, we talk about things…a lot! If you let others help, you will be more educated and more effective. (You'd call this "bouncing things off others.")

Two, we're always learning new things. This lets us discover unique and creative ways to tackle tough people and situations. Each time you learn, you enable yourself to "think outside the box" (or "think outside the planet" as we say in Jurdy World).

Three, we value spirituality. I don't mean religion, but rather a belief that all things work as they are intended to. Believe that your soul is here to work in unison with other souls… difficult ones, funny ones, smart ones and the nuts ones! Taking the time to feel that connection with the universe is not only healing, but uplifting. Nature surrounds you for that purpose. Take the time to do the "spiritual slowdown." You'll be richer for it.

31

Jurdy™

©Jenifer Jurden 06

"If life is one big karate lesson,
watch where you stand."

Jurdy, 2007

(kick it up with others - don't kick them out)

The Human Portfolio

You are your work and your work is you.

Your Current World

You need more pride.

I was blown away by how carelessly and rapidly you move through your work just to say "it's done." You don't take time to check your work or think about how to present it, and then you're forced to take extra time to fix the errors on the back end. You need to invest the time early on to get things right and avoid the last minute, time consuming frenzy.

You interview and hire the wrong people.

Humans inherently default to hiring people just like them. So now you have companies with people who think and work alike. BORING! And you spend all this time finding new hires but then throw them to the wolves their first day. There is little to no direction or guidance.

Good people managers are a rare find.

Most humans in the companies I observed were ineffective managers. They cared most about themselves and yet you put them in charge of other people's careers? Most managers feel comfortable giving only negative feedback and finding fault while not working as hard!

Jurdy's Target World

Get proud, take pride!

If you think about it, the work you do and how you do it speaks volumes about the type of person you are. People are *always* watching, listening and analyzing all you do and the pride you take in your work. This lays the foundation for how well you will be received and valued by co-workers and management. Great work translates into great rewards. Remember, it could be the difference between you and that bigger desk.

In Jurdy World, we take pride in our work and our work in turn builds our pride. The better we do at work, the better we feel at work and success just snowballs from there. Our goal is to do our work right the first time to avoid doing things over. Getting it right the first time allows us to get more done and keeps us moving forward. Our Jurdy World managers are held to very high standards when it comes to the work they and their teams produce. From interviewing and hiring to the actual work they do, they are accountable. The managers work harder and longer than their team members which in turn inspires the team members to work harder and longer! Very cool... and it works.

Focus on quality not quantity! It's not enough to just "do the job," you must also do *the* job well. If you do sloppy work, you'll be seen as a sloppy worker. But if your work is impeccable and perhaps even ahead of schedule, you will fast become that "go-to" person. This person is held in the highest regard because not only are they reliable, accurate and result oriented, they aim to exceed expectations! Here are key Jurdy World tips to *exceed* at work:

- *Make sure it's 100% right.* Even one error can cast that shadow of a doubt on your reputation.
- *Turn your work in early.* This really makes a strong statement that you get things done and make things happen.
- *Provide multiple clean copies.* Think ahead to who will need what … it makes their job easier. Make them look good!
- *Be enthusiastic about the results.* Present your work in person for added impact. Never leave your work on someone's desk… it screams you don't care. Serve it up yourself to get the face time!
- *Ask what else you can do* upon completion of an assignment. Be eager. Management notices.
- *Confirm what others want from you.* Get it right and avoid pie in your face.

Get that "can-do" work ethic! The top 5 show-stopping phrases in your companies are: "I can't do that." "It's impossible." "I can't work overtime." "There's no way." "They'll just have to wait." Stating the impossible makes it impossible for "result seekers" to work with you. In Jurdy World, phrases which don't include *what can be done* are banned from the work lingo. Okay, so how do we do it better? Our top five Jurdy phrases when we respond to challenges are: "Let me see what I can do." "Does all of it need to be done at the same time?" "What options can we come up with." "Can we get extra help?" "We may not get it all done but here's what we know can get completed." At the end of the day, *something* is always possible – even if it's not the full request. Remember, it's all in the delivery. Tell them what can be done, not what *can't!*

Get that reputable reputation! Reputations never follow, they only precede you. If a bad reputation gets to someone before you've had a chance to prove your worth, you'll be deemed worthless. Work independently if given a solo assignment. (Buddies muddy the waters of your successes.) Work hard. Be the first to volunteer for the overtime. The goal here is to make others want you on their team. Be great at what you do, put in the time to do it right and ahead of schedule. Assure its accuracy and show enthusiasm! Now *that's* a Jurdy World reputation to be proud of!!

Hiring the right people allows you to be competitive without being combative. The wrong person in the right job breaks a company down faster than you can say "Uh oh!" Remember, the people *are* the company. People are your biggest asset. Pay attention and spend those hiring dollars wisely.

In Jurdy World, hiring the right people is what takes us such light years ahead of our competition. We ask oddball questions our potential hires couldn't prepare for. We probe as much for their weaknesses as we do for their strengths. We expose them to the realities of our work environment to ensure they want us as much as we want them. The secret to successful hires is realizing that the relationship starts with the interview, not just their first day on the job. And not unlike a marriage, we make sure there is a "good fit" between our candidates and our companies before committing to a relationship.

The interview setting. Where and how you conduct an interview is essential to getting a "true read" on your candidate. In your companies, interviews are usually conducted behind closed doors with the predictable "text book" questions. In Jurdy World, we make the interviewing process as close to the real thing as possible so the candidate gets a feel for the true experience of working there… thus giving us a true read on the candidate. Our interviewing process goes something like this:

Conduct the interview in an open space or open door office. While you might say interruptions are rude during someone's interview, we say they are essential because in reality, workdays are comprised of numerous interruptions. How well the candidate tolerates these interruptions will tell you a lot about them. How well can they get back to what they were saying? How well do they juggle the distractions with getting their information across? Do they show a temper or a willingness to go with the flow? Give them the real thing and watch closely!

The interview questions. The questions you ask in an interview can make or break a good hiring effort. In your workplace, the questions I witnessed were generic and predictable: "What are your strengths?... Why do you want to work here?" In Jurdy World, our questions are designed to get to the real meat of who the candidate is. If you want to hire extraordinary talent don't ask ordinary questions. Instead try these:

- *What are your <u>weaknesses</u>?*
- *How would your previous co-workers describe working with you?*
- *Do you make mistakes?* (If they say no, thank them for coming in and shake their hand goodbye. Everyone makes mistakes and should admit to them!)
- *How would you handle working with an impossible personality?*
- *What if I asked you to work a weekend or overtime?*
- *Would you be willing to actually look at some of the work you'd be hired to do real quick?* (and then if applicable, give them a fast assignment or show them the work and ask for their thoughts. Put them on the spot and see if they can think on their feet.)
- *How well do you take criticism?* (This one really gets them.)

The first day on the job. Humans are notorious for doing a dump and run when the new person shows up for their first day. You spend all this time finding the candidate but then your efforts often stop there. The more you put into the hire, the more you'll get back. Show them, guide them, explain things to them and set all the expectations up front. Invest in the new hires to get the biggest return down the road. In other words, *show them the ropes*.

Humans in the workplace use the term "manager" lightly. You often assign the most inept people this title without considering the impact it has on your work force. I observed managers who were immature, lazy, de-motivating, insulting and just downright negative. Managers in many cases make more money but work less hours than the people reporting to them. You've got it backwards! In fact, many of your managers abuse their role and take things too far.

In Jurdy World, managers are coaches first, and leaders second. They don't have power over others, they know how to influence and develop others. And managers don't manage others, they manage "the efforts" of others. Our managers have *three* distinct rules they follow:

One, their people must succeed for them to succeed.
Two, they must work longer and harder than their people.
Three, they must produce positive results for the company.

Remember: A strong manager makes a strong business.

Managers should only do well when the team does well. A manager is no different than the coach of a basketball team. If the team does well, the coach does well. If the team loses, the coach is perceived as ineffective. Companies should practice the same theory. In fact, managers should be called coaches. They should be positive no matter what, be able to identify talent and develop it and make each person a "go to" person, not just the naturally talented ones.

© Jenifer Jurden 2007   www.jurdy.net

Managers should work harder. It's a pretty simple formula. If the manager is a level above others and makes more money, they should work smarter and harder. The people or teams who report to a manager observe everything that manager does, have no doubt. They watch and listen, and in large part, adopt that very manager's work ethic and their secret to "supposed" success. In Jurdy World, managers get to work early so they are there when their people arrive. They also stay at work until the last person on their team has left for the day. You should see what this does for morale!

Managers should get results. Managers can be loved by their teams and management, but if they don't get results, they are wasting the company's time and energy. By getting results I mean making things happen. In Jurdy World, managers are held to a strict code of expectations that get measured quarterly. In fact, they each receive the "Jurdy Handbook of Management" when they first become managers. (Perhaps I'll publish this next for the human work force.) Each Jurdy World manager is required to achieve the following for success:

- *Motivate each person* to create a winning and happy team.
- *Get to work* before their people arrive and leave after their last person has left. (Particularly on bad weather days!)
- *Produce written goals* for each person aligned with the company's goals. The deliverables should be well defined.
- *Arrange for quarterly team "out of the office" brainstorming sessions* where successes and challenges are flushed out in a fresh environment.
- *Give verbal feedback* as needed and don't forget the positive! The first sentences should always be about what is being done well.
- *Regularly report to upper management* on status and people performance. Manage the dollars and the business.
- *Manage change.* Be able to initiate, anticipate and navigate change and help the team to do the same. Without change, there is no growth.

Above all, managers need to be ethical. If you can't trust your managers, you shouldn't trust them in your business.

© Jenifer Jurden 2006

The Jurdy World recap to success!

... the highlights, the important stuff, the top tips.

(for those of you who want to be sure you got it... or for those of you who weren't paying attention until now)

The following pages easily recap the highlights of this book.
Refer to them, use them and teach them. Then be really smart.

YOUR CAREER –

1. **Don't blame others** – Take responsibility for your career.
2. **Be happy for others** – They will remember you for it.
3. **Sell yourself** – Don't rely on others to do it for you.
4. **Track your accomplishments** – Publish them.
5. **Be visible** – Be seen. Get face time.
6. **Act today what and who you want to be tomorrow.**
7. **Work in teams, not in vacuums** – For optimum results.
8. **Get involved, don't be an outsider** – Volunteer!
9. **Be positive or be quiet** – Be remembered as an optimist.
10. **Model yourself after others who are highly regarded.**
11. *Who are you most like at work? Are they successful?*

_____

_____

GETTING ALONG WITH OTHERS –

1. **Show respect to others** – Particularly management!
2. **Mind your manners, be appropriate** – Even at office parties.
3. **Learn that you have things to learn** – Know-it-alls fail.
4. **Know the personalities you're dealing with:**
   - *We We We's...* It's all about teams. Hang with this group!
   - *Me Me Me's...* It's all about them. Feed their ego to gain ground
   - *See See See's...* It's about just getting the job done. Reward them.
   - *Hee Hee Hee's...* Backstabbers and mean. Fly under their radar.
5. **Avoid gossip** – It will always bite you in the ---.
6. **Treat each individual individually** – What makes each tick?
7. **Motivate yourself, motivate others, motivate management.**
8. *Who is the best motivator you know? How do you match up?*

_____

_____

YOUR HEALTH & ATTITUDE -

1. **Get a life** – Laugh for stress relief and perspective.
2. **Get down time** – Do nothing and enjoy it.
3. **Get to know your family and friends again** – Rely on them.
4. **Treat your bodies to an overhaul** – Get in shape, work better.
5. **Get enough rest** – Don't try to operate without sleep.
6. **Exercise and get active** – It will give you more energy.
7. **Stay in shape once you're in shape** – Make it a routine.
8. **Be mindful of your mind** – Sharp minds get noticed.
9. **Talk things out with others** – Tap into spirituality.
10. **Educate yourself and always be learning something new.**
11. *Think of 2 things you could learn to help you do your job better.*

_____

_____

GETTING YOUR WORK TO WORK FOR YOU -

1. **Take pride in your work** – If you don't, others won't.
2. **Get it 100% right 100% of the time** – Be a star. Don't settle.
3. **Say what you *can* do, not what you can't do** – Find options.
4. **Build a strong reputation** – Care how others perceive you.
5. **Hire the right people** – Really get to know the candidates.
6. **Make each interview unique to the candidate**
   - Ask unanticipated questions
   - Give them true to life surroundings during the interview
7. **Spend time with a new hire** – Show them the ropes.
8. **Assure managers get results for the business** – Bottom line.
9. **Managers are coaches** – Accountable for team happiness.
10. **Managers don't have power, they have influence** – Coach!
11. *Who are the 2 best managers you know? How do you match up?*

_____

_____

BONUS SECTION

Common sense human workplace foibles to avoid (… but let's laugh at them.)

Don't lose your head at work. Use the "24 hour rule" and cool down for a night before responding.

Don't talk just to talk. Have a good point if you want respect.

Don't rely on others too much. Double check everything to avoid surprises.

Don't work until you're insane. Spread the extra hours out.

BONUS SECTION *(continued for your human enjoyment)*

Don't let technology leave you behind. Know the lingo and the products.

Don't stand out in the wrong ways. Look the part and then stand out by being smart.

Don't get too complacent or comfortable in your job. Always be ready for change or a re-organization.

Don't call a meeting if you aren't prepared. Be ready or just postpone it.

BONUS SECTION *(yeah, there's still more!)*

Unless it's your job, don't be on the phone constantly. It will look like you don't have enough to do.

Don't go to work if you can't work. Stay home and get better so you can get productive.

Don't leave important or confidential documents on the copy machine. It won't end well.

Don't get too heated up at work. No one wants to clean up your personal messes, so stay cool!

BONUS SECTION *(it's too fun to put down isn't it?)*

Don't ever steal from your company no matter how small an amount. If caught, this stays with you forever.

Don't be late for work. In fact, getting there early shows your boss and peers that you've got leadership traits!

Don't waste time splitting hairs. Know when to end the meeting and start producing.

Don't be frail or wimpy at work. No matter how you feel, always exude confidence.

BONUS SECTION *(sorry... the fun ends here)*

Don't bug others for stuff you need from them. You can "nudge" but don't bug.

Don't take people and things at face value. Study them first before making any decisions.

Don't ever make enemies. You never know who will be your boss one day.

Don't talk about others in the elevator. You never know who's listening.